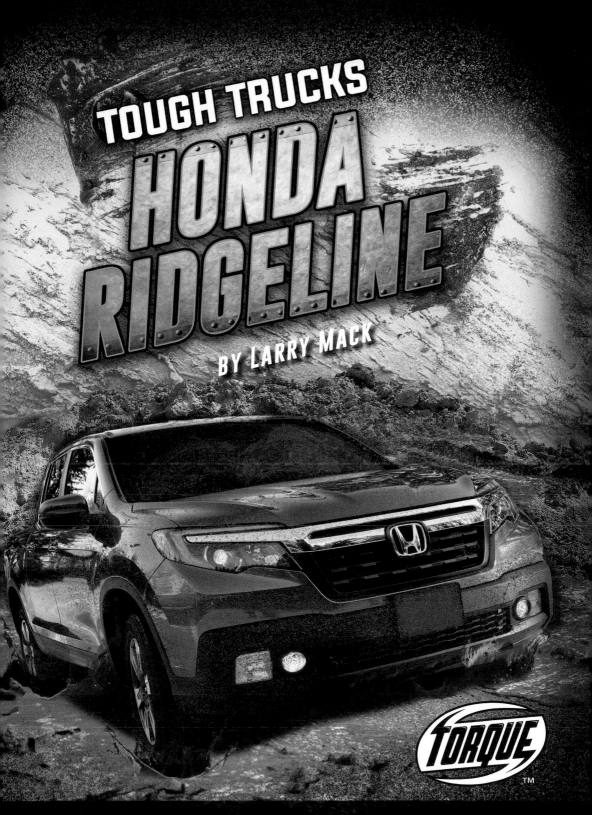

TOUGH TRUCKS

HONDA RIDGELINE

BY LARRY MACK

BELLWETHER MEDIA • MINNEAPOLIS, MN

Are you ready to take it to the extreme?
Torque books thrust you into the action-packed world
of sports, vehicles, mystery, and adventure. These books may
include dirt, smoke, fire, and dangerous stunts.
WARNING read at your own risk.

This edition first published in 2019 by Bellwether Media, Inc.

No part of this publication may be reproduced in whole or in part without written permission of the publisher.
For information regarding permission, write to Bellwether Media, Inc., Attention: Permissions Department,
6012 Blue Circle Drive, Minnetonka, MN 55343.

Library of Congress Cataloging-in-Publication Data

Names: Mack, Larry, author.
Title: Honda Ridgeline / by Larry Mack.
Description: Minneapolis, MN : Bellwether Media, Inc., 2019. | Series:
   Torque. Tough Trucks | Includes bibliographical references and index.
Identifiers: LCCN 2018004997 (print) | LCCN 2018008129 (ebook) | ISBN
   9781626178939 (hardcover : alk. paper) | ISBN 9781681036120 (ebook)
Subjects: LCSH: Ridgeline truck–Juvenile literature.
Classification: LCC TL230.5.R53 (ebook) | LCC TL230.5.R53 M33 2019 (print) |
   DDC 629.223/2–dc23
LC record available at https://lccn.loc.gov/2018004997

Editor: Betsy Rathburn   Designer: Josh Brink

Printed in the United States of America, North Mankato, MN.

TABLE OF CONTENTS

COUNTRY ROADS AND CITY STREETS

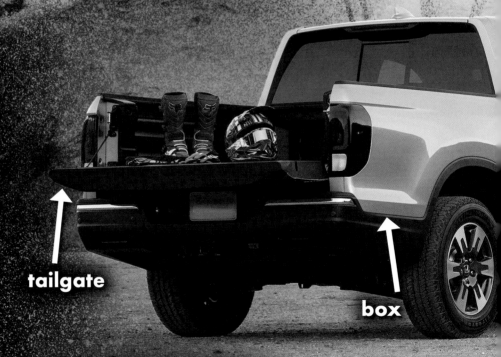

tailgate

box

Two dirt bikes rumble as they turn the corner of a dusty desert road. They are headed for the shiny pickup truck parked at its edge.

The riders open the truck's **tailgate**. They place their helmets into the hidden storage area. Then, they load their bikes into the **box**. It is time to go home!

After the bikes are loaded, the riders climb into the truck. They fasten their seatbelts and take off down the road!

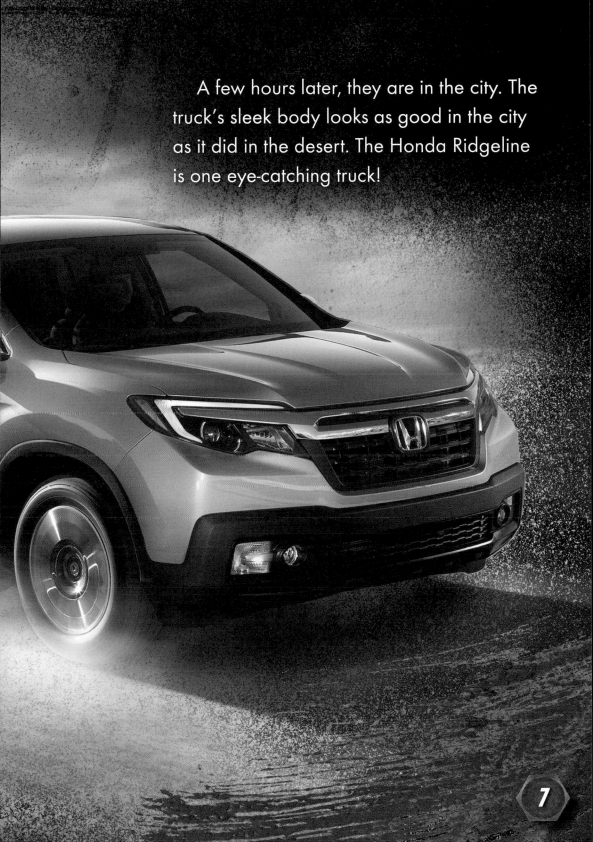

A few hours later, they are in the city. The truck's sleek body looks as good in the city as it did in the desert. The Honda Ridgeline is one eye-catching truck!

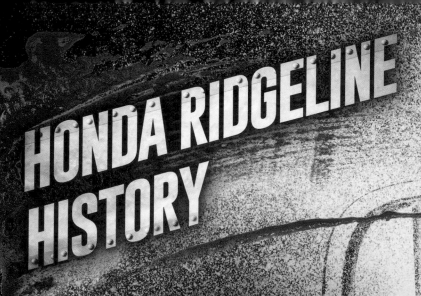

HONDA RIDGELINE HISTORY

Soichiro Honda was a racecar mechanic in Japan. In 1937, he borrowed money to start a company that made car parts. Later, he started a new company called Honda.

Soichiro Honda

1963 Honda T360

Honda became the world's largest motorcycle company after **World War II**. The company's first truck was introduced in 1963. It was a small pickup called the T360.

Honda grew more successful with later motorcycles and cars. The company introduced the Honda Civic to the United States in 1973. This car was popular for its **fuel efficiency**.

1973 Honda Civic

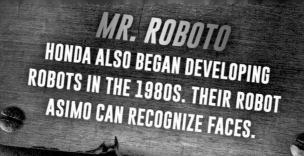

2006 Honda Ridgeline

The company became even larger in the following decades. In 2005, the Honda Ridgeline hit roads. It was a popular truck for Honda fans!

HONDA RIDGELINE TODAY

The second **generation** of Ridgelines came out in 2016. Honda increased the engine's **horsepower**. They also added cool gadgets. These make the trucks safer, easier, and more fun to drive!

POWERFUL RACER

THE ENGINE IN THE RIDGELINE RACE TRUCK CREATES 550 HORSEPOWER. THAT IS ALMOST TWICE AS POWERFUL AS THE ENGINE IN NORMAL RIDGELINES!

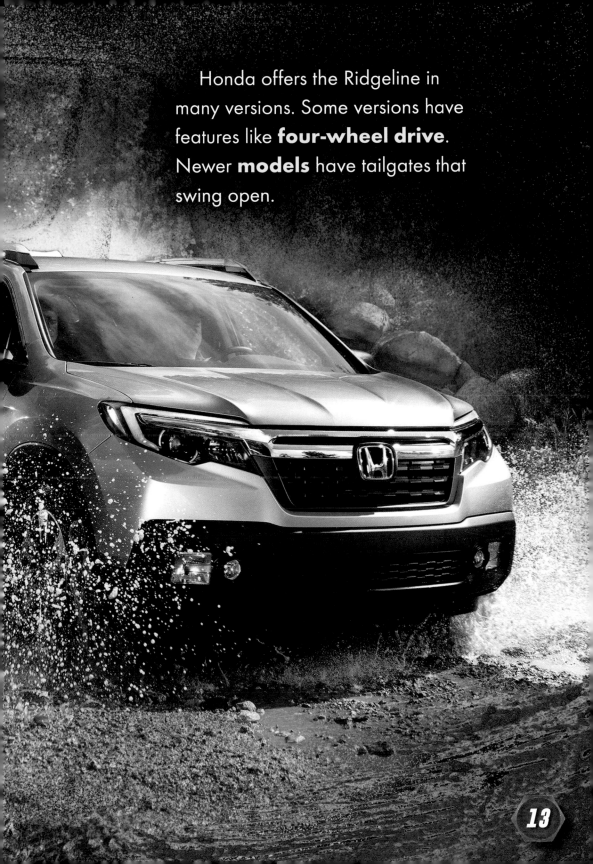

Honda offers the Ridgeline in many versions. Some versions have features like **four-wheel drive**. Newer **models** have tailgates that swing open.

FEATURES AND TECHNOLOGY

The Ridgeline has a **V6 engine**. The engine powers the pickup's big 18-inch (46-centimeter) wheels.

The Ridgeline's body is special, too. The body panels and **chassis** are one piece. This makes the truck stronger, safer, and lighter. It also makes the Ridgeline more fuel-efficient than other pickups.

SMART TRUCK
THE HONDA RIDGELINE HAS SPECIAL SETTINGS FOR DRIVING IN SNOW AND MUD. THE DRIVER JUST PUSHES A BUTTON TO MATCH THE DRIVING CONDITIONS!

3.5L V6 engine

**Honda Ridgeline
Black Edition**

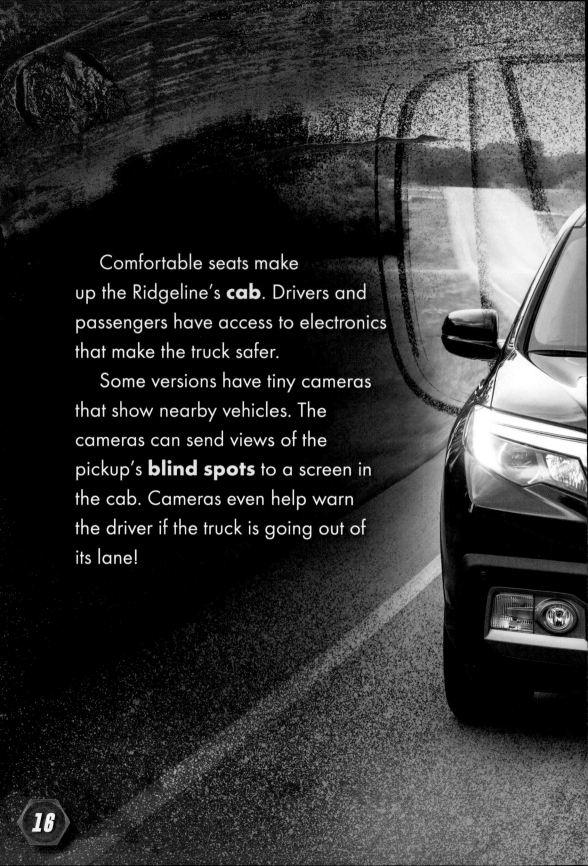

Comfortable seats make up the Ridgeline's **cab**. Drivers and passengers have access to electronics that make the truck safer.

Some versions have tiny cameras that show nearby vehicles. The cameras can send views of the pickup's **blind spots** to a screen in the cab. Cameras even help warn the driver if the truck is going out of its lane!

cab

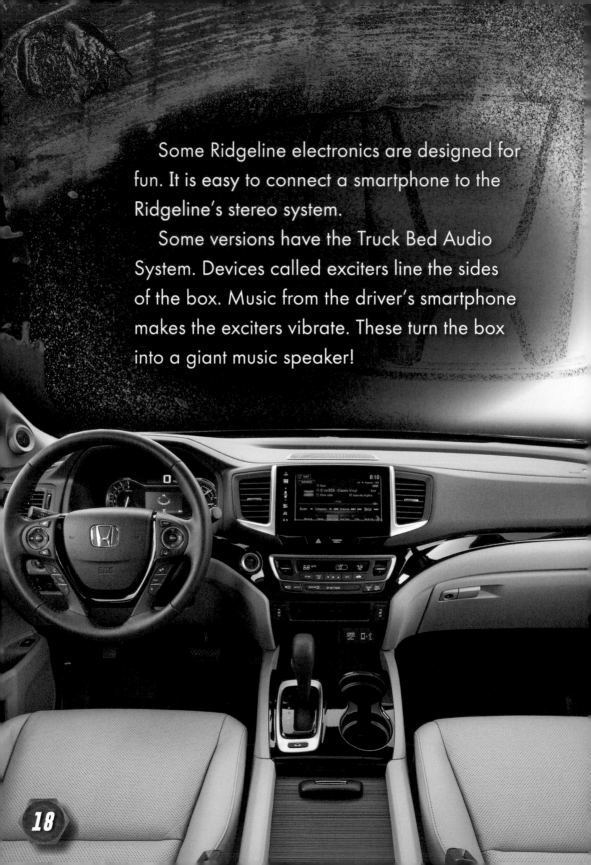

Some Ridgeline electronics are designed for fun. It is easy to connect a smartphone to the Ridgeline's stereo system.

Some versions have the Truck Bed Audio System. Devices called exciters line the sides of the box. Music from the driver's smartphone makes the exciters vibrate. These turn the box into a giant music speaker!

2019 HONDA RIDGELINE RTL-E SPECIFICATIONS

ENGINE	3.5L V6 ENGINE
HORSEPOWER	280 HP (209 KILOWATTS) @ 6,000 RPM
TORQUE	262 LB-FT (36 KG-M) @ 4,700 RPM
TOWING CAPACITY	UP TO 5,000 POUNDS (2,268 KILOGRAMS)
MAXIMUM PAYLOAD	1,499 POUNDS (680 KILOGRAMS)
FUEL ECONOMY	18 TO 25 MILES PER GALLON
CURB WEIGHT	4,515 POUNDS (2,048 KILOGRAMS)
WHEEL SIZE	18 INCHES (46 CENTIMETERS)

TRUCK OF THE FUTURE

Honda Ridgeline owners like their pickups for many reasons. The trucks are safe, comfortable, and fun to drive.

In the future, the truck will only get better. Some experts believe Honda will one day offer **hybrid** Ridgelines. These may help drivers use less fuel. The Honda Ridgeline is a great truck on the dirt and in the street!

TV TIME
ELECTRICAL OUTLETS IN THE RIDGELINE'S BOX MEAN YOU CAN WATCH A BIG-SCREEN TV ANYWHERE!

HOW TO SPOT A HONDA RIDGELINE

HONDA LOGO ON GRILLE

TAILGATE THAT SWINGS OPEN

SLEEK BODY

GLOSSARY

blind spots—areas around a truck that the driver cannot see when sitting inside

box—the area in the back of a pickup where cargo is carried

cab—the area of a pickup in which the driver and passengers sit

chassis—the frame of a truck

four-wheel drive—a feature that allows the engine to turn all four wheels at once

fuel efficiency—the measure of how much fuel an engine needs to create power

generation—a version of a model

horsepower—a unit of measurement used to describe an engine's power

hybrid—a vehicle that uses both gasoline and electricity to drive

models—versions of a truck

tailgate—a door that helps keep cargo inside a pickup's box

V6 engine—an engine with six cylinders arranged in a V shape

World War II—a conflict from 1939 to 1945 that involved many of the world's countries

TO LEARN MORE

AT THE LIBRARY

Bowman, Chris. *Pickup Trucks.* Minneapolis, Minn.: Bellwether Media, 2018.

Mack, Larry. *Ford F-150.* Minneapolis, Minn.: Bellwether Media, 2019.

Mack, Larry. *Toyota Tacoma.* Minneapolis, Minn.: Bellwether Media, 2019.

ON THE WEB

Learning more about the Honda Ridgeline is as easy as 1, 2, 3.

1. Go to www.factsurfer.com.

2. Enter "Honda Ridgeline" into the search box.

3. Click the "Surf" button and you will see a list of related web sites.

With factsurfer.com, finding more information is just a click away.

INDEX

The images in this book are reproduced through the courtesy of: Kelvin Eng/ Wikipedia, front cover (hero); Andrey Kuzmin, front cover (title texture), pp. 2-3 (metal texture), 11 (metal), 12 (metal), 15 (metal), 19 (metal), 20 (metal); Full_chok, front cover (background); xpixe, front cover (top mud, bottom mud); diogoppr, front cover (mud splash); tanuha2001, pp. 2-3 (logo); Kieran White/ Wikipedia, pp. 2-3 (truck); Yulia Plekhanova, pp. 2-3 (background); Honda, pp. 4-5, 6-7, 12-13, 14-15, 15 (engine), 16-17, 18-19, 19, 20, 21 (left, middle, right); roger tillberg/ Alamy, p. 8; baku13/ Wikipedia, p. 9; Joost J. Bakker IJmuiden/ Wikipedia, p. 10; GREGORY SHAMUS/ Newscom, p. 11; sociolgas, p. 21 (metal).